Desi Dad Cookbook

by

Ahmad Babar

Contents

Introduction

Greetings Desi Dads! We know how important it is for fathers to take an active role in cooking for their families. Not only does it allow you to spend quality time with your loved ones, but it also shows your commitment to providing them with nutritious and delicious meals. And who doesn't love a good surprise every now and then? That's why we've created the "Desi Dad Cookbook".

In this cookbook, we have gathered a collection of easy-to-make, authentic Desi & continental recipes that are sure to impress your family and leave them asking for seconds. We understand the busy lives that Desi fathers lead, which is why all of our recipes are designed to be simple, quick, and delicious. From classic dishes like Butter Chicken and Biryani to traditional favorites like Samosas and Green Chutni, we've got you covered.

Whether you're new to cooking or a seasoned pro, these recipes are straightforward and accessible, allowing you to create delicious meals in no time. We've included all of the essential tips and tricks to help you perfect your skills and become a master in the kitchen. From ensuring that the spices are perfectly balanced to getting the texture of your dishes just right, we'll guide you every step of the way.

Not only will you be able to bond with your loved ones over a delicious meal, but you'll also be able to create memories that will last a lifetime. Imagine the look of pride on your children's faces when you serve up a plate of perfectly cooked Butter Chicken or a fragrant pot of Biryani. With this cookbook, you'll have the power to make mealtime a special occasion, every day.

So, get ready to don your apron and roll up your sleeves, because with this cookbook, you'll be able to turn your kitchen into a Desi paradise. Happy cooking, Desi Dads! Buon appetito!

Chicken Tikka Masala

Ingredients:

- ✓ 1 lb boneless chicken breast, cut into 1 inch cubes
- ✓ 1 cup plain yogurt
- ✓ 1 tbsp garam masala
- ✓ 1 tsp cumin
- ✓ 1 tsp coriander
- ✓ 1 tsp turmeric
- ✓ 1 tsp paprika
- ✓ 1 tsp garlic powder
- ✓ 1 tsp ginger powder
- ✓ 1 tsp salt
- ✓ 1 tsp chili powder (optional)
- ✓ 1 tbsp oil
- ✓ 1 large onion, chopped
- ✓ 2 cloves garlic, minced
- ✓ 1 can of tomato puree
- ✓ 1 cup heavy cream

Instructions:

1. In a large bowl, combine the chicken, yogurt, garam masala, cumin, coriander, turmeric, paprika, garlic powder, ginger powder, salt, and chili powder (if using). Mix well and set aside for 30 minutes.
2. In a large pan, heat the oil over medium heat. Add the onion and garlic and cook until softened, about 5 minutes.
3. Add the tomato puree to the pan and cook for another 5 minutes.
4. Add the marinated chicken to the pan and cook until browned on all sides, about 10 minutes.
5. Add the heavy cream to the pan and stir to combine. Cook for another 5 minutes, or until the sauce has thickened.
6. Serve over steamed basmati rice and garnish with cilantro, if desired.

Samosa

Ingredients:

- ✓ 2 cups all-purpose flour
- ✓ 1/2 teaspoon salt
- ✓ 3 tablespoons vegetable oil
- ✓ 6 tablespoons warm water
- ✓ 2 medium potatoes, peeled and diced
- ✓ 1/2 teaspoon cumin seeds
- ✓ 1/2 teaspoon coriander powder
- ✓ 1/2 teaspoon cumin powder
- ✓ 1/2 teaspoon turmeric powder
- ✓ 1/2 teaspoon garam masala
- ✓ 1/2 teaspoon amchur powder (dried mango powder)
- ✓ Salt to taste
- ✓ 2 tablespoons chopped cilantro
- ✓ Oil for deep-frying

Instructions:

1. In a large mixing bowl, mix together the flour and salt.
2. Add the vegetable oil and mix until the mixture resembles coarse crumbs.
3. Gradually add the warm water and knead until a smooth dough forms.
4. Cover the dough with a damp cloth and let it rest for 15 minutes.
5. In a large pan, heat some oil and add the cumin seeds.
6. Once the cumin seeds start to crackle, add the diced potatoes and cook until soft.
7. Add the coriander powder, cumin powder, turmeric powder, garam masala, amchur powder, salt to taste, and chopped cilantro. Mix well and let the mixture cool.
8. Divide the dough into equal portions and roll each one into a thin circle.
9. Cut the circle in half, and roll each half into a cone. Fill the cone with the potato mixture.
10. Seal the edges of the cone with a mixture of water and flour to form a triangle-shaped samosa.
11. Heat the oil in a deep frying pan and gently drop the samosas into the hot oil.
12. Fry until golden brown, approximately 5 minutes.
13. Drain the samosas on a paper towel and serve hot with chutney or ketchup.

Enjoy your homemade Indian samosas!

Chicken Biryani

Ingredients:

- ✓ 1.5 lbs boneless chicken, cut into pieces
- ✓ 2 cups basmati rice
- ✓ 4 cloves of garlic, minced
- ✓ 1 inch ginger, grated
- ✓ 1 onion, thinly sliced
- ✓ 2 tomatoes, chopped
- ✓ 1 teaspoon cumin seeds
- ✓ 1 teaspoon coriander seeds
- ✓ 1 teaspoon turmeric powder
- ✓ 1 teaspoon cumin powder
- ✓ 1 teaspoon garam masala
- ✓ 1/2 teaspoon red chili powder (optional)
- ✓ Salt to taste
- ✓ 2 tablespoons vegetable oil
- ✓ 2 cups chicken broth
- ✓ 1/2 cup fresh mint leaves, chopped
- ✓ 1/2 cup fresh cilantro leaves, chopped
- ✓ 2 cups boiling water
- ✓ 1/2 teaspoon saffron strands (optional)
- ✓ 1 lemon, cut into wedges

Instructions:

1. In a large saucepan, heat the oil over medium heat. Add the cumin seeds and coriander seeds and cook until fragrant.
2. Add the garlic and ginger and cook for 1 minute.
3. Add the onions and cook until softened and slightly golden.
4. Add the chopped tomatoes, cumin powder, turmeric powder, garam masala, red chili powder (if using), and salt to taste. Cook until the tomatoes have softened.
5. Add the chicken and cook until browned on all sides.
6. Add the chicken broth, mint leaves, and cilantro leaves. Cover and let simmer for 15 minutes or until the chicken is fully cooked.
7. Rinse the basmati rice and soak it in water for 15 minutes.
8. In a large pot, bring the boiling water to a boil. Drain the rice and add it to the pot. Cook until the rice is just cooked, approximately 8-10 minutes. Drain the rice and set aside.
9. In a large casserole dish, layer half of the cooked rice at the bottom. Spoon half of the chicken mixture on top of the rice. Repeat with another layer of rice and chicken mixture.
10. If using saffron strands, soak them in a small bowl with 2 tablespoons of warm water for 10 minutes. Sprinkle the saffron water over the biryani.
11. Cover the dish with aluminum foil and bake in a preheated 350°F oven for 30 minutes.
12. Serve the biryani with lemon wedges on the side.

Enjoy your delicious Chicken Biryani!

Butter Chicken

Ingredients:

- ✓ 1.5 lbs boneless chicken, cut into pieces
- ✓ 1 cup plain yogurt
- ✓ 2 tablespoons ginger paste
- ✓ 2 tablespoons garlic paste
- ✓ 2 teaspoons garam masala
- ✓ 1 teaspoon turmeric powder
- ✓ 1 teaspoon paprika
- ✓ 1/2 teaspoon cumin powder
- ✓ Salt to taste
- ✓ 2 tablespoons butter
- ✓ 1 onion, chopped
- ✓ 1 cup canned tomato puree
- ✓ 1/2 cup heavy cream
- ✓ 1/4 cup fresh cilantro leaves, chopped

Instructions:

1. In a large bowl, mix together the yogurt, ginger paste, garlic paste, garam masala, turmeric powder, paprika, cumin powder, and salt to taste. Add the chicken and mix to coat. Cover and let marinate in the refrigerator for at least 1 hour, or overnight.
2. In a large saucepan, heat the butter over medium heat. Add the chopped onion and cook until softened and slightly golden.
3. Add the tomato puree and cook for 5 minutes.
4. Add the marinated chicken and cook until browned on all sides.
5. Reduce the heat and let the mixture simmer for 20 minutes or until the chicken is fully cooked.
6. Stir in the heavy cream and cilantro leaves. Cook for 5 minutes or until the sauce has thickened slightly.
7. Serve the Butter Chicken with rice or naan bread.

Enjoy your delicious Butter Chicken!

Gola Kebab (beef or mutton)

Ingredients:

- ✓ 1 lb ground beef or mutton
- ✓ 1 small onion, grated
- ✓ 2 cloves of garlic, minced
- ✓ 1 tablespoon ginger paste
- ✓ 1/2 teaspoon turmeric powder
- ✓ 1 teaspoon cumin powder
- ✓ 1 teaspoon coriander powder
- ✓ 1 teaspoon paprika
- ✓ Salt to taste
- ✓ 2 tablespoons fresh cilantro leaves, chopped
- ✓ 8-10 skewers

Instructions:

1. In a large bowl, mix together the ground beef or mutton, grated onion, minced garlic, ginger paste, turmeric powder, cumin powder, coriander powder, paprika, salt to taste, and cilantro leaves.
2. Divide the mixture into 8-10 portions. Wet your hands to prevent sticking, and shape each portion into a sausage shape, about 6-8 inches long.
3. Thread each sausage onto a skewer. Repeat with the remaining portions.
4. Preheat your grill or griddle to high heat. Place the skewers on the grill and cook for 4-5 minutes on each side or until fully cooked.
5. Serve the Gola Kebabs with a side of chutney or dipping sauce, and with fresh naan or pita bread.

Enjoy your delicious and juicy Gola Kebabs!

Chicken Seekh Kebab

Ingredients:

- ✓ 1 lb ground chicken
- ✓ 1 small onion, grated
- ✓ 2 cloves of garlic, minced
- ✓ 1 tablespoon ginger paste
- ✓ 1/2 teaspoon turmeric powder
- ✓ 1 teaspoon cumin powder
- ✓ 1 teaspoon coriander powder
- ✓ 1 teaspoon garam masala
- ✓ Salt to taste
- ✓ 2 tablespoons fresh cilantro leaves, chopped
- ✓ 8-10 skewers

Instructions:

1. In a large bowl, mix together the ground chicken, grated onion, minced garlic, ginger paste, turmeric powder, cumin powder, coriander powder, garam masala, salt to taste, and cilantro leaves.
2. Divide the mixture into 8-10 portions. Wet your hands to prevent sticking, and shape each portion into a sausage shape, about 6-8 inches long.
3. Thread each sausage onto a skewer. Repeat with the remaining portions.
4. Preheat your grill or griddle to high heat. Place the skewers on the grill and cook for 4-5 minutes on each side or until fully cooked.
5. Serve the Chicken Seekh Kebabs with a side of chutney or dipping sauce, and with fresh naan or pita bread.

Enjoy your delicious and juicy Chicken Seekh Kebabs!

Chicken Karahi

Ingredients:

- ✓ 1 lb boneless chicken, cut into bite-sized pieces
- ✓ 1 large onion, sliced
- ✓ 2 cloves of garlic, minced
- ✓ 1 tablespoon ginger paste
- ✓ 1 large tomato, chopped
- ✓ 1/2 teaspoon turmeric powder
- ✓ 1 teaspoon cumin powder
- ✓ 1 teaspoon coriander powder
- ✓ 1 teaspoon garam masala
- ✓ Salt to taste
- ✓ 1/2 cup heavy cream
- ✓ 1/4 cup fresh cilantro leaves, chopped
- ✓ 3 tablespoons oil

Instructions:

1. In a large pan, heat the oil over medium heat. Add the sliced onion and cook until softened and lightly browned, about 5-7 minutes.
2. Add the minced garlic and ginger paste, and cook for another 2-3 minutes.
3. Add the chopped tomato and cook until soft, about 5 minutes.
4. Stir in the turmeric powder, cumin powder, coriander powder, garam masala, and salt to taste. Cook for 2-3 minutes until fragrant.
5. Add the chicken pieces to the pan and cook until browned on all sides, about 8-10 minutes.
6. Pour in 1/2 cup of water and bring to a boil. Reduce heat to low, cover the pan, and let simmer until the chicken is fully cooked, about 10-15 minutes.
7. Stir in the heavy cream and cilantro leaves, and cook for another 2-3 minutes.
8. Serve the Chicken Karahi with rice, naan, or pita bread.

Enjoy your delicious Chicken Karahi!

Mutton Qorma

Ingredients:

- ✓ 1 lb boneless mutton, cut into bite-sized pieces
- ✓ 2 large onions, sliced
- ✓ 4 cloves of garlic, minced
- ✓ 1 tablespoon ginger paste
- ✓ 1 large tomato, chopped
- ✓ 1/2 teaspoon turmeric powder
- ✓ 1 teaspoon cumin powder
- ✓ 1 teaspoon coriander powder
- ✓ 1 teaspoon garam masala
- ✓ Salt to taste
- ✓ 1 cup heavy cream
- ✓ 1/4 cup fresh cilantro leaves, chopped
- ✓ 1/2 cup plain yogurt
- ✓ 4 tablespoons oil

Instructions:

1. In a large pan, heat the oil over medium heat. Add the sliced onions and cook until softened and lightly browned, about 5-7 minutes.
2. Add the minced garlic and ginger paste, and cook for another 2-3 minutes.
3. Add the chopped tomato and cook until soft, about 5 minutes.
4. Stir in the turmeric powder, cumin powder, coriander powder, garam masala, and salt to taste. Cook for 2-3 minutes until fragrant.
5. Add the mutton pieces to the pan and cook until browned on all sides, about 8-10 minutes.
6. Pour in 1/2 cup of water and bring to a boil. Reduce heat to low, cover the pan, and let simmer until the mutton is fully cooked, about 20-25 minutes.
7. Stir in the heavy cream, cilantro leaves, and yogurt. Cook for another 2-3 minutes.
8. Serve the Mutton Qorma with rice, naan, or pita bread.

Enjoy your delicious Mutton Qorma!

Mutton Chops

Ingredients:

- ✓ 6-8 mutton chops
- ✓ 2 large onions, sliced
- ✓ 4 cloves of garlic, minced
- ✓ 1 tablespoon ginger paste
- ✓ 1 large tomato, chopped
- ✓ 1/2 teaspoon turmeric powder
- ✓ 1 teaspoon cumin powder
- ✓ 1 teaspoon coriander powder
- ✓ 1 teaspoon garam masala
- ✓ Salt to taste
- ✓ 1/2 cup heavy cream
- ✓ 1/4 cup fresh cilantro leaves, chopped
- ✓ 2 tablespoons oil

Instructions:

1. In a large pan, heat the oil over medium heat. Add the sliced onions and cook until softened and lightly browned, about 5-7 minutes.
2. Add the minced garlic and ginger paste, and cook for another 2-3 minutes.
3. Add the chopped tomato and cook until soft, about 5 minutes.
4. Stir in the turmeric powder, cumin powder, coriander powder, garam masala, and salt to taste. Cook for 2-3 minutes until fragrant.
5. Add the mutton chops to the pan and cook until browned on both sides, about 8-10 minutes.
6. Pour in 1/2 cup of water and bring to a boil. Reduce heat to low, cover the pan, and let simmer until the mutton is fully cooked, about 20-25 minutes.
7. Stir in the heavy cream and cilantro leaves, and cook for another 2-3 minutes.
8. Serve the Indian Mutton Chops with rice, naan, or pita bread.

Enjoy your delicious Indian Mutton Chops!

Daal Makhni

Ingredients:

- ✓ 1 cup black lentils (urad daal), rinsed and drained
- ✓ 1 cup red kidney beans (rajma), rinsed and drained
- ✓ 1 large onion, chopped
- ✓ 4 cloves of garlic, minced
- ✓ 1 tablespoon ginger paste
- ✓ 1 large tomato, chopped
- ✓ 1/2 teaspoon turmeric powder
- ✓ 1 teaspoon cumin powder
- ✓ 1 teaspoon coriander powder
- ✓ 1 teaspoon garam masala
- ✓ Salt to taste
- ✓ 1/2 cup heavy cream
- ✓ 1/4 cup fresh cilantro leaves, chopped
- ✓ 2 tablespoons ghee or oil

Instructions:

1. In a large saucepan, add the black lentils, red kidney beans, 4 cups of water, and bring to a boil. Reduce heat to low, cover the pan, and let simmer until the lentils and beans are fully cooked, about 1 hour.
2. In a separate pan, heat the ghee or oil over medium heat. Add the chopped onions and cook until softened and lightly browned, about 5-7 minutes.
3. Add the minced garlic and ginger paste, and cook for another 2-3 minutes.
4. Add the chopped tomato and cook until soft, about 5 minutes.
5. Stir in the turmeric powder, cumin powder, coriander powder, garam masala, and salt to taste. Cook for 2-3 minutes until fragrant.
6. Add the cooked lentils and beans to the pan and stir to combine with the spices and tomato mixture.
7. Stir in the heavy cream and cilantro leaves, and cook for another 2-3 minutes.
8. Serve the Daal Makhni hot with rice, naan, or pita bread.

Homemade Naan

Ingredients:

- ✓ 1 cup all-purpose flour
- ✓ 1/2 teaspoon baking powder
- ✓ 1/2 teaspoon salt
- ✓ 1/4 teaspoon sugar
- ✓ 1/4 cup warm water
- ✓ 2 tablespoons plain yogurt
- ✓ 2 tablespoons ghee or melted butter
- ✓ 1/4 teaspoon nigella seeds (optional)

Instructions:

1. In a large mixing bowl, whisk together the flour, baking powder, salt, and sugar.
2. In a separate bowl, mix together the warm water, yogurt, and ghee or melted butter.
3. Add the wet ingredients to the dry ingredients and mix until a soft dough forms. Knead the dough for 5-7 minutes until smooth and elastic.
4. Cover the dough with a damp cloth and let it rest for 30 minutes to 1 hour.
5. Preheat a large cast iron pan or griddle over medium-high heat.
6. Divide the dough into 8 equal pieces and roll each piece into a ball. On a lightly floured surface, roll each ball into a thin oval shape.
7. Place the naan in the preheated pan and cook until bubbles form on the surface and the bottom is lightly browned, about 1-2 minutes. Flip the naan and cook for another 1-2 minutes on the other side.
8. Brush the cooked naan with melted ghee or butter and sprinkle with nigella seeds if desired.

Green Chutni

Ingredients:

- ✓ 1 cup fresh cilantro leaves
- ✓ 1 cup fresh mint leaves
- ✓ 2 green chili peppers
- ✓ 2 cloves of garlic
- ✓ 1 inch piece of ginger
- ✓ 1/2 teaspoon cumin powder
- ✓ 1/2 teaspoon coriander powder
- ✓ Salt to taste
- ✓ 2 tablespoons lemon juice
- ✓ 3 tablespoons water
- ✓ 3 tablespoons plain yogurt
- ✓ 2 tablespoons oil

Instructions:

1. In a food processor or blender, combine the cilantro leaves, mint leaves, green chili peppers, garlic, ginger, cumin powder, coriander powder, salt, lemon juice, and water. Blend until smooth.
2. In a pan, heat the oil over medium heat. Add the blended chutni mixture and cook for 2-3 minutes.
3. Stir in the yogurt and cook for another minute.
4. Serve the Green Chutni as a dip or a condiment with your favorite dishes.

Kung Pao Chicken

Ingredients:

- ✓ 1 lb boneless chicken breast, cut into 1 inch cubes
- ✓ 1 tbsp cornstarch
- ✓ 1 tsp salt
- ✓ 1 tsp black pepper
- ✓ 2 tbsp oil
- ✓ 2 large red bell peppers, chopped
- ✓ 1 large onion, chopped
- ✓ 2 cloves garlic, minced
- ✓ 1 tbsp ginger, grated
- ✓ 1 tbsp Sichuan peppercorns
- ✓ 2 tbsp soy sauce
- ✓ 1 tbsp hoisin sauce
- ✓ 1 tbsp rice vinegar
- ✓ 1 tsp sugar
- ✓ 2 tbsp roasted peanuts

Instructions:

1. In a large bowl, mix together the chicken, cornstarch, salt, and pepper. Set aside.
2. In a large pan, heat the oil over high heat. Add the chicken and cook until browned on all sides, about 10 minutes.
3. Remove the chicken from the pan and set aside.
4. In the same pan, add the red bell peppers, onion, garlic, ginger, and Sichuan peppercorns. Cook until softened, about 5 minutes.
5. Add the soy sauce, hoisin sauce, rice vinegar, and sugar to the pan and stir to combine.
6. Return the chicken to the pan and stir to coat in the sauce.

7. Serve over steamed rice and sprinkle with roasted peanuts.

Pad Thai

Ingredients:

- ✓ 8 oz rice noodles
- ✓ 2 tbsp oil
- ✓ 2 cloves garlic, minced
- ✓ 1 large onion, sliced
- ✓ 2 large eggs
- ✓ 1 lb shrimp, peeled and deveined
- ✓ 2 tbsp soy sauce
- ✓ 2 tbsp hoisin sauce
- ✓ 2 tbsp palm sugar
- ✓ 2 tbsp lime juice
- ✓ 1 tsp red chili flakes (optional)
- ✓ 1 cup bean sprouts
- ✓ 1 large carrot, julienned
- ✓ 1/2 cup chopped peanuts
- ✓ 2 green onions, chopped
- ✓ Cilantro, chopped, for garnish

Instructions:

1. Soak the rice noodles in warm water for 30 minutes, then drain and set aside.
2. In a large wok or pan, heat the oil over high heat. Add the garlic and onion and cook until softened, about 5 minutes.
3. Add the eggs to the pan and scramble until cooked.
4. Add the shrimp and cook until pink and curled, about 5 minutes.
5. Add the noodles, soy sauce, hoisin sauce, palm sugar, lime juice, and chili flakes (if using) to the pan and stir to combine.
6. Add the bean sprouts, carrot, peanuts, and green onions and stir to combine.
7. Serve immediately and garnish with cilantro.

Japanese Teriyaki Chicken

Ingredients:

- ✓ 4 boneless, skinless chicken breasts
- ✓ 1/4 cup soy sauce
- ✓ 1/4 cup sake
- ✓ 1/4 cup mirin
- ✓ 1/4 cup brown sugar
- ✓ 2 cloves garlic, minced
- ✓ 1 inch ginger, grated
- ✓ 2 tbsp cornstarch
- ✓ 2 tbsp water
- ✓ Sesame seeds, for garnish
- ✓ Green onions, chopped, for garnish

Instructions:

1. In a large bowl, whisk together the soy sauce, sake, mirin, brown sugar, garlic, and ginger.
2. Add the chicken to the bowl and marinate for at least 30 minutes or up to overnight.
3. In a small bowl, whisk together the cornstarch and water to form a slurry.
4. In a large pan or wok, heat a small amount of oil over medium-high heat.
5. Remove the chicken from the marinade and reserve the marinade.
6. Cook the chicken in the pan until browned on both sides and cooked through, about 8-10 minutes.
7. In a small saucepan, bring the reserved marinade to a boil.
8. Stir in the cornstarch slurry and continue to cook, stirring constantly, until the sauce has thickened, about 5 minutes.
9. Serve the chicken with the teriyaki sauce, garnished with sesame seeds and green onions.

This flavorful and savory teriyaki chicken is a staple of Japanese cuisine and is sure to please everyone at the dinner table. Whether served over rice, noodles, or vegetables, it's a delicious and easy-to-prepare meal that's sure to become a regular in your meal rotation.

Tiramisu in a Cup

Ingredients:

- ✓ 2 egg yolks
- ✓ 2 tablespoons sugar
- ✓ 1/2 cup mascarpone cheese
- ✓ 1/2 cup heavy cream
- ✓ 1/2 teaspoon vanilla extract
- ✓ 2 tablespoons coffee, cooled
- ✓ 2 tablespoons coffee liqueur
- ✓ 12 ladyfingers
- ✓ Cocoa powder for dusting

Instructions:

1. In a medium bowl, whisk together the egg yolks and sugar until light and frothy.
2. In a separate bowl, beat the mascarpone cheese, heavy cream, and vanilla extract until soft peaks form.
3. Fold the mascarpone mixture into the egg yolk mixture until well combined.
4. In a shallow dish, mix together the coffee and coffee liqueur.
5. Dip each ladyfinger briefly in the coffee mixture and place 3 of them at the bottom of 2 cup glasses.
6. Spoon half of the mascarpone mixture over the ladyfingers in each cup.
7. Repeat the layers of ladyfingers and mascarpone mixture in each cup.
8. Cover and refrigerate the cups for at least 2 hours or overnight.
9. Before serving, dust the top of each cup with cocoa powder.

Chocolate Chip Brownies

Ingredients:

- ✓ 1 cup unsalted butter, cut into pieces
- ✓ 2 cups granulated sugar
- ✓ 4 large eggs
- ✓ 1 teaspoon vanilla extract
- ✓ 1 1/4 cups all-purpose flour
- ✓ 3/4 cup cocoa powder
- ✓ 1/2 teaspoon baking powder
- ✓ 1/2 teaspoon salt
- ✓ 1 1/2 cups semisweet chocolate chips

Instructions:

1. Preheat your oven to 350°F (175°C) and grease an 8x8 inch square baking pan.
2. In a large saucepan, melt the butter over low heat. Remove from heat and stir in the sugar.
3. Add the eggs, one at a time, to the sugar mixture, beating well after each addition. Stir in the vanilla extract.
4. In a separate bowl, whisk together the flour, cocoa powder, baking powder, and salt. Gradually add the dry ingredients to the sugar mixture and mix until just combined.
5. Fold in the chocolate chips.
6. Pour the batter into the prepared baking pan and spread evenly.
7. Bake for 25-30 minutes, or until a toothpick inserted into the center comes out clean.
8. Allow the brownies to cool completely in the pan before slicing into squares.
9. Enjoy your delicious chocolate chip brownies!

Thank You Desi Dads

Dear Desi Dads,

I hope this message finds you well. I just wanted to take a moment to express my sincerest gratitude for choosing to purchase my cookbook "Desi Dad Cookbook." It means the world to me that you have trusted me to provide you with easy and delicious recipes to cook for your families.

I am truly grateful for your support and for helping me to share my love of cooking with others. It has been a dream of mine to publish a cookbook and I couldn't have done it without you.

I hope that you have found the recipes to be both delicious and easy to make. I would love to hear any feedback or suggestions that you may have, as I am always looking for ways to improve.

Thank you again for your support. I am humbled and grateful to be able to share my passion for cooking with you.

Wishing you all the best,

Ahmad Babar

Printed in Great Britain
by Amazon

20692699R00025